BEST
THOUGHT,

WORST
THOUGHT

Other Books by Don Paterson

Poetry

>*Orpheus*
>*Landing Light*
>*The White Lie: New and Selected Poetry*
>*The Eyes*
>*God's Gift to Women*
>*Nil Nil*

Aphorism

>*The Blind Eye*
>*The Book of Shadows*

Editor

>*New British Poetry* (with Charles Simic)
>*Don't Ask Me What I Mean:*
>>*Poets in Their Own Words* (with Clare Brown)
>*Last Words* (with Jo Shapcott)
>*Robert Burns: Selected Poems*
>*101 Sonnets: From Shakespeare to Heaney*

BEST
THOUGHT,

WORST
THOUGHT

⸘

On Art, Sex, Work, and Death

Aphorisms

Don Paterson

Graywolf Press
Saint Paul, Minnesota

Publication of this volume is made possible in part by a grant provided by the
Minnesota State Arts Board, through an appropriation by the Minnesota State
Legislature; a grant from the Wells Fargo Foundation Minnesota; and a grant from
the National Endowment for the Arts, which believes that a great nation deserves
great art. Significant support has also been provided by the Bush Foundation;
Target; the McKnight Foundation; and other generous contributions from foun-
dations, corporations, and individuals. To these organizations and individuals we
offer our heartfelt thanks.

MINNESOTA
STATE ARTS BOARD

NATIONAL
ENDOWMENT
FOR THE ARTS
A great nation
deserves great art.

Aphorisms in *Best Thought, Worst Thought* were originally published in *The Book of
Shadows* (Picador, 2004) and *The Blind Eye: A Book of Late Advice* (Faber and Faber,
2007), both published in the United Kingdom.

Published by Graywolf Press
2402 University Avenue, Suite 203
Saint Paul, Minnesota 55114
All rights reserved.

www.graywolfpress.org

Published in the United States of America

ISBN 978-1-55597-505-0

2 4 6 8 9 7 5 3 1
First Graywolf Printing, 2008

Library of Congress Control Number: 2007940217

Cover design: Kyle G. Hunter

for Nora

Contents

Foreword

On the morning the Barbarians wandered through the gates, everyone in Rome had their feet up and was reading a foreword.

≬

The aphorism is a *brief* waste of time. The poem is a *complete* waste of time. The novel is a *monumental* waste of time.

≬

The aphorism: too much too soon or too little too late, but never just enough for the time being.

≬

Yes I *know* Marcus Aurelius or Vauvenargues or Chesterton has already said this, and far more elegantly; but let's face it, you weren't listening then either.

≬

The aphorism will often contain one italicised word; this denotes its magnetic North, not its direction.

❧

Key: read *I* for *he; R.* for *S.; no one* for *you; it* for *I.*

❧

The shorter the form, the greater our expectation of its significance—and the greater its capacity for disappointing us. A book of aphorisms is a lexicon of disappointments. The form's only virtue is its brevity; at least the reader cannot seriously hold that it has wasted their time.

❧

The aphorism is nobody speaking to nobody; it's less read than eavesdropped upon. God knows, it's barely even *written:* I disown them immediately.

❧

Despite our attempts to imbue them with some flavour, *any* flavour—aphorisms all turn out so ... generic; they all sound as if they were delivered by the same disenfranchised, bad-tempered minor deity.

❧

The aphorism is the rational articulation of a fleeting hysteria.

❧

S. has written a *comprehensive* book of aphorisms. He has made a vast list of subjects, then sat down and composed his brilliancy on each of them—even those on which he had no opinion, until that very moment.

❧

How many aphorists *does* it take to change a lightbulb? How many aphorists does it take to *change* a lightbulb? ... And so on with our little antipoetry, our ear to the strongbox of the line while we work the combinations, trying the italics on one word, then the next, until we hear something weaken inside ...

❧

A book of aphorisms makes no pretence to engage the reader in any sort of dialogue; to judge by its tone of relentless asseveration, it *has no opinion of them*. What the reader feels is a kind of *ultimate* contempt, that of ink for the human, the mineral for the animal.

֍

Z. has numbered his aphorisms. Now he has added a *cumulative* disappointment.

֍

Poetic truth occurs at that point in the steady refinement of a form of words where they cease to be paraphrasable, but have not yet become purely oracular. Also, perhaps, a definition of the aphorism, its talentless, tone-deaf brother.

֍

Allowed myself a smile this morning at a letter innocently referring to 'my love of the aphoristic form'. Heavens—do you think if I really had a *choice,* I would write *this?* We occupy the margins through fate, not allegiance.

֍

The difference between the aphorism and the poem is that the aphorism states its conclusion first. It is a form without tension, and therefore simultaneously perfect and perfectly dispensable. There is no road, no tale, no desire.

꙳

Here is a very bad aphorism for the purpose of illustrative quotation.

꙳

Tried to rewrite this book as less self-important; gave up, realising that was its only virtue.

꙳

Reading a book of aphorisms diligently in the sequence they appear makes about as much sense as eating a large jar of onions diligently in the sequence they appear; and no one should try to finish either in one sitting.

꙳

Notes on a few aphorists:

Canetti: he did not really understand the aphoristic form. In an intelligence like his, this should tell us something of the . . . obscurity of the skill. 'Rarity' might imply it had a value.

Chesterton: the only really great aphorist in English. Halifax is okay, but all the rest—Hazlitt and (curiously) Wilde excepted—are *wits*. The Anglophone embarrassment in regards to the unilateral assertion—which it cannot help thinking of as a subset of 'wisdom literature'—began very early. This it sees as the sole preserve of the holy books; all other attempts at it are laughed away uncomfortably, on the grounds, ultimately, of their seedy human provenance. You would think such a culturally ingrained self-hatred would make the English ideal aphorists. However you can be over-qualified for the task.

Cocteau: he would have been the greatest, but he was far too happy. The dominant harmony and black dissonance supplied by heterosexual self-loathing are the only things I really miss in Barthes, too.

Heraclitus: to read him for the first time is like digging a hundred knives from the ground, nearly all of them still gleaming.

Kraus: too much spleen over sense, and Marx's fatal attraction for rhetorical chiasmus, which is always fake; only forms can be placed in such symmetries, never concepts. And to have affected Schopenhauer's and Nietzsche's *misogyny*, of all their attributes—and this in a genuine lover of women.

Jabès: a great *writer*, but as an aphorist a queer cocktail of rabbinical proverbialism, French blur and poetic overstatement. Contrary to popular belief, there is nothing *self-evident* about the aphorism at all. Within the form, the axiom and the crazy assertion are the same waste of breath.

La Bruyere: a lexicon of human prejudice. Still useful.

La Rochefoucauld: in an old Penguin Classic edition of his work, a superbly bad-tempered back-cover blurb used him to demolish a stupid contemporary critic. Any writer who can be set so easily to his own defence still earns our respect.

Leopardi: I wish we could suppress this adolescent habit of ours of automatically conferring genius upon even the latest of early deaths.

Lichtenberg: German *concision?* He deserves even more credit than we give him.

Neitszche: all his famous contradictions disappear as soon as you remember to read him as *literature,* which is not obliged to be coherent. Nevertheless, while I believe in an absolute separation in reading the life and the work, I find myself making a single, sentimental exception for lunacy in the philosophers, which still somehow discredits them.

Pascal: more and more he reads like Confucius, i.e. an axiomatic redundancy. This probably pays him the highest compliment; every discipline needs its Euclid.

Porchia: possibly the greatest, as almost no one has read him.

St. Thomas Gospel: the Nazarene Cynic laid bare, but somehow St. Thomas still comes out of it better.

Stevens: amateurism is generally a huge advantage to a poet, but this led him only to write the first half of his aphorisms. He omits the *proof.* For the true amateur the slightest literary obligation smacks of a journalistic deadline.

Valéry: if he has one fault, it is that you could always tell he composed his aphorisms horizontally. They taste a little too milky at times, a little too much of sleep.

Cioran: something like Nagarjuna's Western reincarnation. The Buddha, let's remember, *required* our scepticism; Cioran, possibly alone amongst European writers, refined it to attain a kind of terrible, insomniac enlightenment. Like Borges, he managed to turn a European tongue against itself to approach ideas that (unlike Pali, say) it had no right to—and somehow contrive their ghostly appearance, like the animated figures in a zootrope. To read him openly as a Westerner is thus to be a little reprogrammed. No wonder that he is considered, in this age of the pseudoscience, no philosopher, and absent from almost all contemporary accounts of the subject. He wrote only in obsolete genres. By comparison, everything else seems to be already haunted by its own critical refutation, immediately backed into punctilious consistency, supporting references, and an irrefutable (i.e. wholly circular) systematism before it has even begun to articulate its position.

Weil and Arendt's almost inadvertent dalliances apart, women have so far found very little use for the aphorism; far and away the most troubling indictment we can serve against *any* form.

❨

I no longer mean all of these. I meant them once. Some of them *only* once.

❨

Anything that elicits an *immediate* nod of recognition has only reconfirmed a prejudice.

❨

Whatever else, each aphorism also speaks death to the system. That is to say *my creed,* could such a thing exist.

❨

The more obscure the activity, the more certain the opinion of the critics. I would never have suspected the aphorism of having so many *exact* definitions ...

❧

There is a makeweight of lies or conjecture in any statement longer than a sentence, longer than a breath, longer than that which can inhabit the present moment.

❧

A poem is a form of words that advertises its own significance; no more, no less. So with the aphorism, the difference being that *all that exists of it* is the advertisement.

❧

Of course you don't like all the aphorisms. I don't like all of *you.*

❧

To induce a horrific paralysis of boredom in the reader, in the compass of *one sentence* ...

❧

Of *course* all these amount to nothing. Their collation might be my error; their aggregation, however, is yours.

❧

The lapidary coldness of the aphorism assuages a grief or a grievance far better than the poem. It erects a stone over each individual hurt.

❧

My new book arrived, and I had no idea who had written it. Or at least I now understood *why* I had written it: to expel the last man. Forgive the author of this book; but as you can see, I could live with him no longer.

❧

I would make her the Clodia, the Laura, the goddamn *Beatrice* of the aphorism. Now *there* was a gratitude I would have to explain to her.

❧

Why so many aphorisms on aphorisms? Only an ant can correct the manners of an ant.

❧

Fragments, indeed. As if there were anything to break.

❧

The aphorism is already a shadow of itself.

Best Thought, Worst Thought

Falling and flying are near-identical sensations, in all but one final detail. We should remember this when we see those men and women seemingly in love with their own decline.

❧

Traditionally, the defining moment in a man's life arrives when he looks in his shaving glass and finds his father staring back; but there is a day so much more terrible we rarely speak of it—when he catches himself naked in a full-length mirror and sees his *mother* . . .

❧

All that moves is ghost.

❧

Whenever he saw someone reading a bible, he would spoil it for them by whispering, 'He dies in the end, you know.' I'm always tempted to do the same to anyone I see consulting their diary.

❦

I run into a coeval for the first time in ten years. He has become monstrously fat. I tell him, truthfully, that it is a perfect delight to see him.

❦

There were times, moving slowly inside her in the dark, when I would pause, and realize *I was not there*. Only the movement again restored some flicker of allegiance to the here-and-now from which we had all but been exempted.

❦

In my adult life, the time I have actually lived inside the present moment would amount to no more than a single day. If only I could have *lived* it as a single day; it would have thrown its light into all the others, like a brazier in a dark arcade. Instead I find my way by sparks, and what they briefly made visible.

❧

A mercy, I suppose, that it ended. Any deeper intimacy with each other's anatomy would have involved a murder.

❧

A perfectly *human* abyss: 'You felt so close just then. . . .'
'I did?'

❧

I was terrified when I suddenly realized her entire conversation took place in inverted commas. She didn't dare *mean* a thing.

❧

Just as the tongue can no longer taste salt if all it tastes is salt; just as a certain stimulant will eventually clog up the synapses until it ceases to work on the brain—so the lover's body becomes slowly desensualised through its familiarity. Without its continual jittering saccade, the eye would be blind; it sees only by difference. When we cease to triangulate, the world disappears. As soon as we take another lover, and know another shape in our hands again, another form lying below or above us—our partners become desirable again. If we were creatures only of pure desire, this would solve everything.

ɋ

When I was one or two I was obsessed with the lack of features on my parents' faces—the two eyes, the one lonely mouth: I would weep for them, for their blankness. I dread, now, to think of where I had just come from.

ɋ

Writers often end up humourists if they read in public too often. Barring the odd and worthless snort of self-congratulation, laughter is the only *audible* response we can ever elicit. The silence of the unbearably moved and that of the terminally bored are indistinguishable.

❧

The most efficient lies take only two forms: the truth in all but one detail, or a complete untruth. Anything between is amateurism: you are making the fatal mistake of *enjoying yourself.*

❧

When I'm drunk, the ghosts of all my old lovers file through me one by one; I realize I had never stopped loving them, only buried them alive in me.

❧

My work is the deferral of work, which exhausts me; the actual work I barely notice. As a result I never really feel like I'm working, a happy enough state of affairs for all but the Calvinists, for whom it is *an exact torment.*

≀

Suddenly there was nothing I could do to impress her. All the brilliant discursion, the sublime compliments, the poems and songs I laid at her feet . . . I began to fear the worst: that if I was loved at all I was *loved for myself.*

≀

When I first learned that Bach preceded Mozart I was completely incredulous. All but the most naive among us accept that literature doesn't progress, but we've always held out higher hopes for music, as if the species might somehow hitch a ride on it.

≀

We live in a human dream; being one in which everything appears purely in the guise of its human utility, and held in place by its human name. Names are small and sinister metaphors which restrict, absolutely, the *use* of an object. Our eyes open to this madness every morning, and at night we dream within the dream; whole lives are spent without as much as a ripple of doubt on its surface. But when the object is allowed to shrug off its name, it begins the long road back to its own mystery—and on finally reaching the core of its own estranging fire, radiates until the whole world is unified by it. The rose or the paperclip; either could open the path back to our awakening.

❧

Already, deranged by love, he was thinking of revenge— even if he could not decide or even locate the offence. Then it struck him: given her addiction to the vanishing trick, to her oblivions . . . he would *memorialise* her.

❧

I no longer fantasize about being caught. I have long since apprehended myself; I am disappointed in me enough for everyone.

❡

There is no day. The sun interrupts a continuous night. Our ancestors were correct: the sun abandons us.

❡

Everything in nature we don't understand we once called miraculous.

❡

The speed of email allows us to develop sensitivities previously unknown to the epistolary arts. In the number of kisses appended to the foot of each message, we quickly learn to read not only the fluctuation of affection, but its disguise, its reigning in, and its cruel or flirtatious withdrawal. Connoisseurs of the *x,* after our affair was over, we tacitly settled on three: this exceeded the perfunctory, but didn't sign any inappropriate . . . revivals. Once, in a fit of enthusiasm, I added four. *I think you think I'm someone else*—the acid, instant response.

❡

No matter how beautiful it is, if it appears in the wrong month: kill it.

❡

Mediocre art is far worse than bad. Bad art does not waste our time.

❡

Every friendship demands loyalties that require the small betrayal of another. It is impossible to have more than ten real friends and be true to them all. Twenty and not a single one can trust you, nor should.

❧

Terrible dream last night. I am standing at the window watching a great storm—the trees thrash around, the flowers flatten themselves to the earth, the grass dances wildly. Forgetting that one should never answer the telephone in a dream, I take a call, and learn that M. has died. I go outside and everything is still in complete frenzy, but there is not a single breath of wind.

❧

Entire *years,* in total, thinking about sex. But then: entire years spent asleep. Heigh ho.

❧

Almost everything in the room will survive you. To the room, you are *already* a ghost, a pathetic soft thing, coming and going.

❦

Since it's only the idea that charms in conceptual art, the actual presence of the art itself affords us no greater revelation. On the contrary, it reduces the imaginative possibilities of the concept to precisely one. Besides, conceptual art just sounds like a contrived synonym for *the book*.

❦

The Age, God help it. One occasionally takes its accurate pulse. This week, in love again, I turn *instinctively* to solace myself not in the Song of Songs, or Burns or Sappho . . . but Roland Barthes.

❦

Good ideas prompted, bad ideas willed.

❦

He was a man of such wide-ranging ignorance . . . it had
real subtlety, depth, *reach* . . .

❧

We were packing to leave the chalet; it was the first clear
evening since we'd arrived. The sun was levelling, like a carpenter's eye, on the coast; and suddenly the effaced shape
of every barrow and fort and souterrain rose from the fields
and hills in its black cloak, and the whole land, its whole
human history, was readable again. I began to wonder if
our own last night might not be the same, the shades of all
our past lives standing up again, to be briefly reckoned and
dismissed.

❧

As soon as we refocus our criticism *ad hominem* to *ad librum,*
our enthusiasm for everything but praise deserts us, and we
pass over the bad books in silence.

❧

He is an almost worthless man; therefore we *know* our kindness to him a true charity. Worthless, but useful.

꧁

I would never claim to have her measure. However she gave me mine. My gratitude is . . . complex.

꧁

There are some of us most attracted where we know we'll be most coldly dismissed, for whom the turned face— being precisely where we came in, with *God forsaking us to the world of men*—is actually our deepest possible nostalgia, and hell.

꧁

We lie down when the length of our shadows becomes intolerable.

꧁

We learn from history and repeat it cheerfully. History does not caution; it sanctions.

᠗

Only the insecure age valorizes the individual voice; partly because it fears it has no collective voice, and partly so that it might encourage its radical artists towards a speech far easier to identify and suppress.

᠗

I find some recordings by the guitarist John Abercrombie almost infinitely replayable; the reason is that the strings lie utterly dead under his fingers, the way they do only with a complete beginner. Next to vocalists, players of stringed instruments have the most direct means of sound production, and therefore find it hardest to avoid the sin of *expression*. Singers and violinists make up a disproportionate number of the musicians I find perfectly insufferable.

᠗

Those men who masturbate while thinking of *nothing;* who don't even remember their *own* birthdays; who make bookless train journeys where they do nothing but stare into space . . . no society is ever short of them. The worst atrocities are derelictions not of the spirit but of the imagination. Babi Yar and Nanking were supreme failures of the human imagination. If you can imagine how a raped child feels, then your identification is instantaneous; you banish the idea before it even becomes a *thought.* Naively, I used to think that this reflex was fractured only in the psychotic.

❧

Thirty years and the name of this 'titan of the scene'—I read here—is completely forgotten. Such was his conviction of his own genius, he felt his work needed no *argument;* instead, all we got was vatic pronouncement, the last word on the matter. Argument is the church of the poem. His voice boomed away but made not a single echo.

❧

I have one enemy, and by never naming her I torment her continually. Were she a man I might do the reverse.

❧

He seemed to have lost so much in translation I began to suspect him of having *gained*.

❧

Poetry is a mode of reading, not of writing. We can read a poem into anything.

❧

Some people achieve their humility by prayer and fasting, some by great charitable works. My own method is to behave in public like a complete moron every three months or so.

❧

Don't mistake petrifaction for inner strength. The walking dead often appear impossibly stoical to us.

❧

We turn from the light to see.

❧

Technically, speech is a very complicated form of song.

♪

No fury more righteous than that of a sinner accused of the wrong sin.

♪

In some Neanderthal part of me, every husband poses an affront.

♪

Appalling that so many of my imagined triumphs still take place before my second-year school assembly, who will finally vindicate me . . .

♪

Each time I reveal to someone my last deceit, I am compelled to perpetrate another. Something of me always concealed from *everyone,* I will always know some small part of ghosthood.

♪

How often I've mistakenly returned to an early draft of a poem, and made the same tiny changes I had already made a month earlier. Though I take this less as a token of the work's smooth march to its imago than an identical state of *shortfall;* others would have done better. Everything might start heading straight towards my dream of it, but is slowed and then halted at the limit of my contract, my karma, my luck.

❧

There was no point in dedicating myself to besting the rival suitors. Unlike them—*superior* to them—I knew her real worth; I spent my time looking over my shoulder for Odysseus.

❧

Terrible description in the newspaper today of a woman watching her child fall, fatally, from a high playground chute. *It was if everything went into slow motion. . . .* No—time had not slowed; she had hesitated, our human instinct being to watch first and act second. Can you imagine a lioness in such a paralysis of *spectatorship?*

❧

The priestly good looks, the almost ostentatiously plain wife. . . . His saintly expression a reproach of sorts, insofar as you had to suspend dealings in your usual currency— you wouldn't dare tell the mildest story against a *soul,* knowing he'd never take your side. There was a time when I used to think that such a man brought out the best in people. But since he rejects *all* allegiances, which are only forged against something or other, we all leave his company perfectly disgusted with ourselves.

꙰

Roll on the biotech phase, please; if only to stop all this *sweating . . .*

꙰

What my cabal look for: quick eyes. (The quick brain is another matter.) When we see those, we immediately acknowledge a brother or sister under the curse of the present moment.

꙰

Disconsolately toying with my $40 plate of saffron risotto in some ramshackle private club in the company of a comic librettist, an agent, and a publisher of erotic literature—the C-list to which I obviously aspired so keenly—I knew as much abasement as I would have found in Gurdjieff's commune, in the driving rain, standing in the bottom of a hole I had been digging for a week, a hole I had been forced to dig *for no reason*. The lessons we need we find anywhere.

❧

Seventy years. But your childhood was an infinity. What fools we were to sign up to time.

❧

If I knew that, like Picasso, I might remain sexual *to the end*—I'd probably have made no attempt at reform. So much 'selfwork' is just the dignified accommodation of one's own decrepitude.

❧

A pianist I know had a hopeless and purely neurotic dependency on sheet music, and couldn't play a note without a chart in front of him. After months of trying to cure himself, he was finally able to take just a blank sheet of paper on stage, though he never managed to dispense with this crutch entirely. I hardly use my reference library at all, yet I'd be lost without it. Ideally, I'd have the walls covered with empty books: not just the usual grammars and rhyming dictionaries, but *The Book of Next Lines; A Lexicon of Cadence; Metaphor Conversion Tables; Rare and Unused Images*...

♪

Though we acquire an air of inviolate religiosity in our solitude, nothing makes us less human than a solitude interrupted; specifically, the monophone treble obscenity of the *William Tell* Overture on the mobile phone of the guy opposite me on the train, his huge red spectacles, his yelled bonhomie.... I find myself praying that his next call will bring him news of the death of his mother.

♪

In bed she had the trick of indicating everything with complete explicitness, while still managing to communicate entirely by way of euphemism and babytalk. . . . Like the 1,000 names of God, as if the world would vanish if she were to articulate the *cunt*. Suddenly I understood the mystery of the palladium.

҂

Women are better than men.

҂

Anal sex has one serious advantage: there are few cinematic precedents that instruct either party how they should *look*.

҂

Translated verse is usually given away by the strenuous informality of its delivery. As if you had presented your passport and visa before anyone had asked for it: such behaviour only arouses suspicion.

҂

Zero-valent: of an atom that cannot combine with any other. Those days when she felt herself undergo a kind of centripetal collapse, spinning to almost nothing, like a star in its last days, a nothing with a terrible weight at its exact and more exact centre.

❧

I cannot read more than a line of anything Hartley Coleridge or John Clare wrote, even a scrap of correspondence, without being reminded of what Rilke felt towards dogs: he loved them so much he could not bear to be in the same room as them, so appalled was he by 'these creatures . . . we have helped up to a soul for which there is no heaven', and their curse of feeling *everything.* John Clare, John Clare, even his name flays me.

❧

Any series of brilliancies, like those million exposures we suffer cycling down a sunlit avenue, begin by exhilarating us and end in nausea and disorientation. As mature readers, the fireworks might still dazzle, but it's the longueurs that sustain us.

❧

Too late for everything; not too late for anything; we flip between death and eternity, and either way nothing gets done.

❧

After a long period of reflection, he decided that he was in fact right yet again.

❧

Whenever we return with music from our dreams, it retains its beauty; the beautiful line of verse, though, oxidises on its exposure to daylight, and turns to gibberish before our eyes. No better proof that music pays its line far more deeply into the unconscious. Poetry is the music of consciousness.

❧

I spoke to a man whose meditational practice, for one entire month, consisted of visualizing his loved ones as skeletons and putrifying corpses. It did indeed allow him to live within the present moment all the more authentically, at the very flickering cursor of its transience. Unfortunately, one year on he could still not make love to his wife.

❧

The untarnishable brilliance of lost work. . . . I remember a sequence of comic stories I completed when I was eight years old, and thought very highly of; then my horror when, a year later, I realized I'd mislaid them. Even now, I have the feeling they would have secured my reputation.

❧

When I turn away from a man and woman she grows wings and he grows horns. I counter the feeling by speaking well of him immediately: *Yeah—nice guy, nice guy, nice guy* . . . my spell against demons. Against the wings I have no protection.

❧

It now transpires from an analysis of Einstein's brain that, as we suspected, he was less an exemplary specimen than a freak; *upon the shoulders of mutants.* . . . Any other species would have smelled him a mile away, and torn him limb from limb at birth, or left him out for the jackals and vultures; they all possess a perfectly sensible terror of innovation. Only a doomed race could prize it.

❧

Amazing the insouciance we learn to affect in the face of the worst thing. Every evening, part of me still wants to rush into the street screaming 'Jesus, can't you people *see*? It's getting *dark*...'

❧

If you were offered one hour or two, would you really choose two? Now: work backwards.

❧

W. miscalculated. He thought he was overexposed, and would be valued for his rare appearances. Within a year they had forgotten him.

❧

We're forever reading atrocities as mere omens; anything to do nothing a little while longer.

❧

To renounce not *the* self, but *your* self; somehow a very
different proposition.

❧

Rejection quickly breeds an unnatural viciousness of style.
Nothing is so conducive to a lyric and contemplative art
as early publication.

❧

If only art were a matter of luck, of very occasional discovery, like those absurd rubies and emeralds and goldseams
that turn up from time to time in the Outer Hebrides. Then
we could dispense with the *artist* . . .

❧

I am berated by a young gunslinger of a drama critic for my 'naive and passé symbolism'. In my next play, a young gunslinger of a drama critic is yanked from the audience, hung and disembowelled in the first scene. I take a deep satisfaction in the thought that even he—however naive and passé he may feel it to be—will find in this no trace of the symbolic whatsoever.

֍

After the events that befell T.—his tragedy was inconceivable, *exceptional*—my immaculate friend did not know how to behave when the subject arose. The situation was absent from her book of protocols. Instead she adopted a robotic neutrality, from which vantage she could observe our shamed and inarticulate flailings. In that moment I saw through her completely.

֍

Why is it I mark the passage of time in my friend's faces with such horror, and in my own with such equanimity? And why do so many women I know suffer the inverse curse?

֍

My project of memorising all the wildflowers of Scotland is
going remarkably well; last week, a rare kind of butterwort,
a pyramid orchid, an eight-petalled wintergreen . . . all
part of the grand plan. Soon I'll be as dead to them as I am
already to the poem and the song; I shall have increased
my *immunity*. At times like this, I begin to understand the
passions of the early anatomists.

)

A stark choice that night: do as she wanted, turn up at her
place, fuck, and inevitably contract the vicious flu she's
carrying, or make my excuses and stay home. Inevitably,
the former. I loved her; besides, I found it intoxicating
to think that I was infecting myself so . . . voluntarily, and
denying the virus its usual satisfaction in seeking me out.

)

All my teachers have been women. Although several men
have taken me aside for an hour to tell me things they know.

)

I read a definition of the word 'solid': *something which retains its shape;* and find myself immediately terrified by the *wilfulness* of objects.

❧

This morning I was dreadfully constipated: not a situation in which, mercifully, I often find myself—but *Jesus . . .* three-quarters of an hour, my forearms bracing the walls like Samson, attempting to gain one further degree of leverage. . . . When the breakthrough finally came, suddenly and with some violence, I suffered the momentary conviction that I had expelled some vital gland or organ. God knows, the municipal statuary of a less prudish race would reflect something of the feats of raw heroism daily enacted in the narrow room. But now, my belt fastens easily, and I'm a little lighter, a little closer to heaven. . . . Having made my votive offering to gravity, gravity relaxes its grip a little. Why did they never place this time amongst the canonical hours? Surely we're more air and fire now than ever.

❧

B. thinks and talks on his feet more brilliantly than anyone I know. I'm always consoled by the reflection that this facility has had the effect of eroding, to the point of extinction, any allegiance he had ever felt to the truth.

❦

In all art, the function of the ego is to drive you to the gig, then keep the van ticking over while you perform without it. Those who fail to do so are easy to identify: they all *shake.*

❦

The only pure suicide is self-strangulation; everything else requires the world as an accomplice. Best was Yogananda's *mahasamadhi*—announcing his departure at the dinner table, and raising his third eye to the crown chakra; such acts implicate nothing else in the universe and are surely committed with no karmic consequence. Perhaps that is the *only* such act.

❦

The drawn curtains in the morning, brightening and darkening like some savage commentary on the fickleness of the human mood.

ʔ

Amazing that the chess-clock never found a more general application. A more enlightened society would have made it as indispensable to conversation as shoes to walking.

ʔ

Strange ceremonies no-one told you you would have to observe. The first lover to die on you. You've made love to a dead woman; the white limbs that were folded round you only last year are already rotting into the earth. You *must* have missed something the last time, some sign, some undertone of *départ* to the proceedings.

ʔ

I was delighted to read in a biography of Adolfo Cerceda, the great Argentinean magician, that 'he survived surgery for a malignant tumour on the lungs, and on his recovery embarked on a world tour, this time changing his name to Carlos Corda'. I immediately saw that there were two or three occasions in my life when a better instinct would have compelled me to act in the same way.

❧

Gravity fluctuates.

❧

A few superstructural facial muscles, that business with the thumbs, a certain delicacy over the matter of cannibalism . . . otherwise no difference worth the name.

❧

Like a fool, I let her know she was on my mind *all the time.* Specifically I was telling her that I *haunted* her; then wondered why the news appalled her so.

❧

Time + consciousness = foreknowledge of our passing. Our only *unique* gift; that we can act knowing, in some sense, that we are already dead.

§

I'm *terrified* of my euphorias. Influenza or despair is a day away.

§

The trees in winter, those exact diagrams of all our dead yearnings.

§

Time heals so well it erases us; we *are* its wounds.

§

The present tense in English is too sibilant to be of much use to poets.

§

That night I ground on, replaying in my mind the first scenes of our lovemaking. It was for that earlier woman I cried out; or for that time when, in the infinite tenderness of our regard, we seemed almost to create one another, to lift each other up into the light . . . before our looking turned into mere *exposure:* that cycle of quotidian betrayal, that hunger that leaches all the mystery from a face, like the colour and perfume from a bottle of scent left too long in the sun.

❧

If we *really* believed a word we said, then—like Socrates, Jesus, Buddha—we would just think aloud. But as small artists, we're morbidly concerned with the dissemination and preservation of the text—from bribing our reviewers and securing our book-club deals, right down to fretting over the stitching and the acidity of the paper. The real prophets always know their words will be carried for them, and are carved into the tablets as they hit the air.

❧

Less is pretty much the same.

❧

No email for an hour. The *bastards.*

❧

Only the incremental advance is consolidated.

❧

Though it seems impossible to believe that My Lai was *ever* (I read here) a 'sleepy village' in South Vietnam, or Thalidomide an anti-emetic, so it must have been. No name is guaranteed its innocence forever. Right now, in your immediate line of sight, there will be one thing—a postcard, a foodstuff, a brand-name—whose apparent inviolate banality will become a horror within your lifetime.

❧

I've noticed that whenever I feel compelled, *for no good reason,* to look at my watch, it's almost always ten to three. Why on earth should I lose always track of the day at this point, as if time itself had slipped a cog? We all know the imp of accidie, who strikes as the sun reaches its zenith; but there are others—*personal* demons—who sit upon certain angles of the clock-hands, as patiently as a vulture on a rock. God knows what *they* are preparing for us.

❧

Consistency, whether of argument, opinion, or 'voice', is only a virtue in the individual opus. Only sentimentalists and the terminally insecure demand that ouevres or *lives* should aspire it.

❧

All true poems are fugitive, being embarrassed by their human source.

❧

Inconveniently, books are all the pages in them, not just the ones you choose to read.

❧

I came home. I had grown sick of my accent.

❧

My admiration for him was too high, and destroyed any chance we might have had of friendship. Every email to him I drafted and redrafted into idiocy, solecism and quixotic affectation. I began to resent him, to devise ways I might discredit him, *depose* him . . . and then understand why he had been wary of me from the start.

❧

Like every other literary critic, Bloom credits the writer with far too much interest in literature. Such as it exists, the Anxiety of Influence is mostly a business between contemporaries. The tensions are all sibling, not Oedipal.

❧

Met P. last night for the first time since she left the firm. She could barely summon the breath to deliver the weakest greeting. Which is where I started with her—invisible, useless, to which state I find I have been promptly and summarily returned. I curse myself for having begun to think well of her. Then I forgive myself: this benign amnesia of mine is just what separates us.

❧

Difficult to understand how such kindness and such a pure vanity could coexist in the one man; clearly, it's more than just the Sisyphean project of clearing his conscience. It would almost be enough to restore my faith, if I only knew in *what*.

❧

He has made a career of his immaculate surface. To hear him order a drink or receive a compliment is to witness a marvel of tact and eloquence; but now everything in the world disappoints him. Though he has become so vitrified, so *deeply* surface—he will not crack, but shatter.

❧

The sex was utterly straightforward, being, for once, a direct means to an end. Couples should not say *we were one,* when they mean *we were nothing.*

❧

Always an error to make someone profess what they will not volunteer—especially in love, where the spontaneity of its declaration is all the language ever holds of it.

❧

Such is E.'s need to be loved, he experiences the casual indifference of a stranger and a snub from his closest friend as the *same torment.*

❧

The lyric efflorescences of youth and old age are only partly mysterious: they are the only two occasions where one can work outside the shadow of criticism. The young poet cannot anticipate it, and the old poet need not.

❧

Our empathies have to be set to the correct aperture. An hour ago, I interrupted my writing to take coffee in the front room; the arm of an old chair had come loose, and appeared to be raised in a gesture of helplessness. . . . I was overcome with a ridiculous sensation of pity, and almost had to check myself from dashing over and helping the thing to its feet. Then the aching lidless stare of the window, the huge weariness of the walls under their weight of books, the carpet's torture of knots, the hundreds of pounds of tension driven into every string in the wretched piano . . . it seemed to me that we'd filled every natural thing with our own torment.

♩

X's honest and atrocious vice is that she values only what is valued for her. She is so attuned to the tiny hourly fluctuations in your celebrity, you can read them off her like an altimeter. There are days when she would throw herself at your feet, others when you could not get her attention if you fell down dead at hers.

♩

The proverbial *white-man-steal-my-soul* refusal of the 'primitive' when faced with a camera lens is less a naive misunderstanding of the photographic process than a deep and correct intuition that all photographers are bastards.

⸮

We feel nothing only under general anaesthetic. I've heard it said that the mere existence of those superb lacunae negates the possibility of an afterlife. I disagree—though they probably show that there is nothing in the next life that will have any currency in *this*. Who knows what angelic conversations we were forced to hand over at customs, before our climb down into the recovery-room.

⸮

The capacity for suffering is proportionate to the suffering; for some, a slight discomfort is as intolerable as passing a kidney stone. Hence the writer's sincere belief that his cramps and boredom qualifies him to animate the worst things that have ever happened to us.

⸮

I try to write rejections of meticulous kindness. Some are sent sincerely, others insincerely, and only I know which. No: *all* are sent sincerely . . . the bad poets are mollified, the talented encouraged, and everyone's happy. It seems unnecessarily cruel that those perennially snubbed by the muse should have to endure a further rebuff from an opinionated nonentity having a bad morning. Hell, some of my *best friends* are talentless.

❧

The sadness of old shoes. Putting them on again, I suddenly remember all the old friends I haven't seen for ages; and then *why*.

❧

A correction made to work more than five years old is less a revision than the cancellation of another man's opinion.

❧

I realized why I could never have married her: when she fell asleep, she put on a coat of lead. No man ever felt so alone as one who spent a whole night with B.

❧

In any other religion one would be shaken by a master's failure—so what is it about the falls from grace of Chogyam Trungpa and Sogyal Rinpoche that seem to *validate* their teaching? Just as the destruction of the Bamiyan Buddhas was a glorious lesson in transience; a reminder that there is no one worth following, only paths.

❧

A style is a strategy of evasion.

❧

Only the dead have a past. As long as we breathe we can be called to account for everything.

❧

I began to relish—to venerate and luxuriate in—that long five-second amnesia as I came to; that gap where, though conscious, we have not yet remembered our bereavement or terror or mad love; where we perceive that our enrolment in the world of pain is in fact entirely voluntary.

❧

The car says *I am the master of my destiny;* the train says *we're all in this together.* I might doubt the second, but the daily carnage testifies to the absolute untruth of the first.

❧

Looking back through the notebooks . . . in certain paragraphs, I seem so much older than I am now; yet two years later the same hand is executing nothing but idiocies. We must hope that something advances in what we forlornly call the *meantime,* and that the soul has its own universities.

❧

Sometimes I wonder if there is an invisible amanuensis on hand at the beginning of our love-affairs, scribbling down the improvisations of the first few hours. Too often it seems that they provide the entire script of the melodrama to come, from which we soon find ourselves incapable of straying a word.

≀

We were meant to make a child and did not allow ourselves to, over and over again. In the end our lovemaking could not shake the taint of *mortification*; of all the things, of all the things.

≀

Mercifully, there is always one earlier writer who seems to scupper our chances of originality. The truly original are unreadable: Joyce became so as soon as his debt was paid to Ibsen.

≀

At the extremes of sexual behaviour, the difference in the projects is still apparent: men are frequently trying to bludgeon themselves into insensibility, women trying to bludgeon themselves into feeling something.

⸮

The reader may be witness to the exchange, but can never participate in it; poetry, in the end, is a private transaction between the author and the Void. The poem is firstly a spiritual courtesy, the act of returning a borrowed book.

⸮

Art can almost be defined as the practice of solving scientific problems without recourse to scientific method. The distance between the stars is traversed only by the artistic imagination; the Bird of Paradise flutters into life in the hands of a bored sailor. The trisection of the angle, employing only a straight edge and a pair of compasses, is, according to Wantzel's irrefutable proof, perfectly impossible. The solution, of course, is to discard the instruments and execute it freehand.

⸮

Sympathetic proof of hylozoism: imagine a stone lying on a beach, undisturbed for fifty years; impossible to think that, walking by, we could pick it up and throw it into the sea, and that it could feel *nothing* . . .

ॽ

I can never think of the time I spend idling in railway stations as lost; it's a waiting liberated from the three temporal vices of regret, anticipation or boredom, the weak echo of that bliss spent between lifetimes.

ॽ

The most erotic things that can be done to you are those that are driven by the purest selfishness on the part of your lover. Charity, on the other hand, is the great anaphrodisiac.

ॽ

I would lie for hours, foetal and agonised with boredom, because—I now learn from my mother—she had taken my books away, having realised being sent to my room was no punishment at all. In the next twenty years I spent more time accumulating books than reading them. Now two lifetimes couldn't read them, or four trucks take them away, or a hundred mothers. Though that one revelation was enough to frighten me off seeking the roots of my other manias.

໒

The insane enthusiasm of a nursery gardener who prunes his roses long before they flower, even the very buds . . . the brutal aesthetic of the bare branch and the thorn . . . to think what a vicious, perfect bloom this strain would immediately bring forth were we simply to *allow* it!

໒

It's a singularly bizarre phenomenon that after the first encounter, the face of the beloved-to-be cannot be retrieved. In our mind's eye, we hold the dinner-table of the previous evening, and though we can sweep from guest to guest, fixing in turn the thin-lipped novelist, the drunken critic, the accountant and his horse-faced wife—however desperately we try to call back her features, there she sits, her face as perfectly bright and blank as if she had spent the entire evening with a mirror held up in its place.

❧

If I do not constantly evince an attitude of self-disgust, it's due to nothing more than a lack of stamina.

❧

If we expect our work to survive our death even by a single day, we should stop defending it this minute, that it might sooner learn its self-sufficiency.

❧

In hell even the trees are not blameless. *Particularly* the trees.

≀

My absolute blind fury at J.'s obituaries, as he denied me
the profound pleasure of being jealous of him any longer . . .
though even in death, I could still discern the cast of ambition in his face. No doubt he's already making his way up
the infernal ladder, and has risen to some subaltern of the
demonic.

≀

In that short walk to the bathroom at three in the morning,
I realized that, caught at the right hour, I would have little
trouble giving up the flesh. I regarded myself as a perfect
stranger; I was no more than a ghost with a full bladder.

≀

Our names should be lengthened a little after our demise, by the lovely matronymic of death . . . we'd then appear in the conversation of our friends and enemies with our signature cadence gently altered, discreetly informing strangers of our change of status.

❧

Every motive, being a different admixture of *every* desire a man or woman possesses, is almost infinitely complex. The failing of all legislators: their inability to see that no one ever acts for one reason alone.

❧

Every morning the writer should go to the window, look out and remind himself of this fact: asides from his own species, not one thing he sees—not one bird, tree or stone—has in its possession the name he gives it.

❧

Hell is an enforced solitude, heaven a voluntary one.

❧

Once, on a long train journey, she taught me to *sign*. It was itself a cruel mime of a request, one she knew to be nearly impossible for me: to pursue her with silence.

❧

The worst atrocities are committed by the absolutists, who don't understand that dishonourable circumstances challenge you to behave with more honour than ever.

❧

Our most grievous error is to think our incarnation some kind of cosmic privilege. We fall into time as a dead leaf into a river.

❧

Reality is just the name that we give to everything that happens to face up.

❧

In art, the only true crime of ignorance is the rediscovery of the cliché. The mark of genius, on the other hand, is its innovation—being the disclosure of what we hadn't known we'd *always* known.

ꝗ

To leave the page covered, and the silence intact; to *enforce* that silence in the reader's life for the duration of the poem ...

ꝗ

Sentimental art often tries to provoke emotions of which we should already be in high possession. What kind of poetry *should* be made for those who require more than flat testimony to be moved by an Auschwitz?

ꝗ

Dying, he's more embittered than ever. As if even his soul had become disgusted with him, and gone ahead alone.

ꝗ

Don't delude yourself that this watery, carbon-based arrangement will persist any longer than necessary. Having failed to locate the soul in the heart, liver, or pineal gland, in a hidden corner of the hypothalamus, or in some probability-field in quantum space—we nonetheless still host it, or the dream of it, and it will set up house just as happily in the motherboards of our scions.

❧

My obsession with computers (what an infancy they're in, and how it *charms!*) is a kind of nostalgia for the future. I long to be half-man, half-desk.

❧

Sleeping with your own muse is an unpardonable breach of literary protocol. But to sleep with a friend's, and tell him about it, is to do him the greatest favour as an artist. I would think.

❧

She was not comfortable with the idea of him alone in her house, less for those secrets of hers he might discover than for the lack of them: the lack was, in fact, her worst secret.

↲

All our instruments are accurate, except the clock. The clock holds up two sticks in the air and draws a conclusion.

↲

Most people are convinced that the path of the departing spirit is distinguished by its scatter of holy detritus (they are forever producing bits of shiny rubbish as evidence of his recent passing); but the one thing of which a god is incapable is fragmentation. The path he has taken is distinguished only by its godlessness. When we stumble upon anything—a bottle of wine, a poem, a poor suburb, a railway platform—that is incontestably the worst of its kind, we know for certain that we have picked up the trail again.

↲

In all beautifully expressed tautologies there is a grain of gold that is surplus. This reliable alchemy applies to all the arts that obey the chrysometric laws, that cut with the golden blade. Philosophy, which cuts with the silver, and works on isometric principles—always falls a grain short. The true poem picks up the gold thread of the hem of the robe of the departing spirit, the glittering clew in the dark woods that will lead us back into the light. The true philosophy delineates the precise nature of its own failure. Therefore, knowing the exact form of *deus absconditus,* we can recognise the godless trail when we stumble across it, and start our pursuit.

ʔ

In her, I realised I had finally given myself up to what I always professed was my true study: *The Interpretation of Silence.* I think perhaps I'd fancied it a fusion of psychoacoustics and critical theory. Immediately I was immersed in Hermes Trismegistus and Aleister Crowley.

ʔ

I have no more ambition for this book than that some day someone will be lying in bed and read out a single line— and that their companion will turn away from them in silence . . .

❧

The sea rehearses all possible landscapes, the sky all possible seas. But the land is a lexicon of frozen hells, and some of us remember.

❧

The language of the angels and of the blessed consists of a single verb, possessing an infinite number of tenses, moods and conjugations. In the language of the damned, every word is a part of speech entirely unrelated to any other; this tongue is the subject of enforced study for those wretches, who, under the scourge of the infernal grammarians, are condemned forever to the memorization of vast and endless textbooks. The two languages are, of course, precisely the same, the only difference being that this knowledge is withheld from the latter party.

❧

The *emphasis* is all wrong; the tale of his life will read like
a great book underlined by an idiot.

❧

Critical theory—a whole subject devised for no other
purpose than the stimulation of underemployed or un-
employable intellects—is incapable of accepting a straight-
forwardly *boring* solution to anything, regardless of how
correct it might prove. It would contradict its status as a
pastime.

❧

Schopenhauer is correct when he asserts that a new face
always shocks us; but it's not the unfamiliarity that's
terrifying—on the contrary, it's the fact that part of us
invariably seems to recall it.

❧

The better part of etymologies lie forever buried from sight.
Words are locked tombs in which the corpses still lie
breathing.

❧

Rusted to the shape of their ideology, the brains of most political demagogues are like a stopped clock; the most dangerous limit their public appearances to twice a day, knowing that they'd be revealed as lunatics at any other hour.

❧

Poetry is the word in silence. Only a poem can consist of one word.

❧

Forty next year. Excellent; that's broken the back of it. Officially, *time will be short.* I can stop pretending that I will ever read George Eliot, that one day every woman will love me, that I find Mozart anything but a huge bore . . .

❧

The gods knew that fane-building was the first step towards their banishment. They are always absent from the temples. What we love about churches is their perfect emptiness.

❧

There is one thing, at least, which everyone regards as the dullest point of common knowledge, the details of which—by tact, providence, but most likely chance—have been withheld from you. So you will discover, too late in the day, why your house was sold to you so cheaply, or the *real* ingredients of the communion host, or that all left-handed males are culled in their fiftieth year.

❡

He only saw value in those who reminded him of himself. His coterie was a hall of cracked and warped mirrors.

❡

I love the way we all suddenly stop traducing our enemy when we hear they have a cancer or have suffered a stroke. If only we could always keep in the front of our minds that we are *all* dying.

❡

The true avant-garde cultivate the territories others merely stake out. They are, furthermore, the real subversives among us, since they never draw attention to themselves through the crime of originality.

⸶

The poet's only consolation is the thought that somewhere, right now, there is a man or woman of infinitely greater intelligence making a complete idiot of themselves as they labour over the composition of a simple couplet.

⸶

Taking a lover often solves the sexual difficulties of a marriage as it becomes pointless to imagine yourself *elsewhere*.

⸶

In the true artist there is no more progression than in the true art.

⸶

There are men and women who talk so seamlessly of themselves you wonder when they managed to listen long enough
to have acquired the power of speech in the first place.

꙳

We grow into our prophesies. Often it is the simple embarrassment of having told everyone we will leave our lover
that gives us the courage to do so; but this example calls a
deeper system from the shadows. Usually we must open up
the path before we can follow it, the air standing—all too
often—solid against us. On those occasions we send out the
god in ourselves, and follow his empty trail to our salvation.
This is why transition so often feels like abandonment.

꙳

The first procedure of good style is the inversion of the form
in which the idea occurred to the thinker.

꙳

Most relationships that begin in deceit end the same way. Our inamorata will never forget the duplicity of which she knows us to be capable. That knowledge soon becomes an expectation, the expectation becomes a prophesy; and in the end, most prophesies compel their own fulfilment. No better example of the way in which karma operates *within* our lives, as well as across the interstices.

❧

Music has the most exact *science* of all the arts. When we hear a note in our heads and attempt to replicate it with our voice or on the piano, our nearest miss is the most disastrous choice we could have made; someone else will come along and hit a note a whole fifth out, with far less discordant consequences. In no other art is this the case— the use of the near-synonym, or the slightly inappropriate pigment, jars only with those deeply attuned to the medium, who perhaps already perceive it as a form of music, a form of pure vibration.

❧

Dinner, and the usual dreadful updates—L's cancer, P's accident, M's stillbirth. . . . Yet the only thing that draws a real gasp from me is the news that X's library has burned down.

)

God's demise: a suicide, surely, if all those reports of it had observed the first poetic imperative, the consistency of the conceit. In which case (before we enter in to more delightful speculation, such as what new limbo he had to prepare for himself in advance) what exactly was his *method?* Though having tried and failed with his starry ligatures and inhaled nebulae, it was no doubt the one thing of which he found himself incapable. The best he could manage was to *fake it*—and being in possession of the one thing he could envy, we were the first to be duped. We are, in fact, his suicide note.

)

To the man who has heard nothing but Bach, everything else he subsequently hears puts him a little in mind of Bach. Bad critics often conceive of similarities that owe nothing to the works themselves and everything to the paucity of examples they have to draw on; their ignorance insists on them.

*

The world disappointed me as soon as I got here. I'm proud of having *lost no time.*

*

We could easily have evolved eyelids thick enough to keep out the light, but we still need to see the shadows fall across it. We're not yet *safe.*

*

One thing all adulterers will tell you: the dreaded return to the marital bed turns out to be such a simple and easy deception, it stands as a far more grave indictment on the spirit than the original misdemeanor ever was.

*

The successful impersonation of intelligence often leads to more original thought than the casual operation of the real thing, as it better comprehends the artifice of the idea—and is therefore not constrained by any attempt, unconscious or otherwise, at *naturalism*.

❧

I considered myself immune to the sirens of suicide, until one morning I somehow managed to alert myself to a grievous sea-change; the idea had just crossed my mind *casually*. Since that moment I have been roped to the mast of myself.

❧

I knew, in the end, that I could addict her to nothing, to no vanity, to no compliment, to no pain—and that this had always been my only strategy. In all matters of love I had never amounted to more than a *pusher*.

❧

I kissed her first in a doorway in Victoria; I kissed her last in a doorway in Victoria. No city allows us to haunt ourselves like London, to contrive such insane symmetries, to find ourselves yet again—years later, *seemingly against all odds*—at the same tiny coordinate in its vast districts. We turn the corner, and the light will suddenly break in on a dark hall, filled with our crossed swords, our mouldering trophies, our ragged tapestries.

❧

Just as men can fuck better on a full bladder, it's better to write with some part of the mind preoccupied with matters other than those immediately at hand; in matters where there is no *real* urgency, it's often worthwhile importing one arbitrarily. I'm most likely to deliver the line I have waited for all morning five minutes before I have to run for a train.

❧

Desire is the inconvenience of its object. Lourdes isn't Lourdes if you live in Lourdes.

❧

No matter how intolerable an event was, it only has to be repeated three times for you to invest it with a little nostalgia.

❧

There can be no such thing, in our human experience, as seamless progress. The suicide's descent from Beachy Head will have its lighter moments; even the road to hell will have stretches more bearable—which we will succeed in construing as more *pleasant*—than others. We're cursed by these, since they continually give rise to hope.

❧

Silence is our only bravery. If 'literary courage' isn't an oxymoron—perhaps it only consists in realising that you've had your last word on the subject and leaving it at that.

❧

As a compositional practice, music is easily superior to poetry in that it can be exercised at will. The composer is often detained in nothing more than the business of making a single large and subtle calculation—the emotion consequently registered in the heart of the listener having, at no point in the process, necessarily been felt in his own. This is unthinkable in poetry, yet more often than not— whatever the agonies or raptures of the poet—the reader is left dry-eyed and perfectly indifferent. But to have felt *nothing,* and *still* devastate an audience; that sensation is probably as close to divinity as we will get.

ℐ

Man is only a biological interlude in a much longer narrative, but *knowing* the fact of his intermediacy between the mineral and the bodiless seraphim makes his condition a sentence, a term. No wonder we count the days the way we do.

ℐ

Cioran talks of the shame of not being a musician. He should have been grateful he never bore the disgrace of being merely an *average* one.

ℐ

A poem is a little machine for remembering itself.

)

If we know we will forgive at some point in the future, we should forgive now; if we intend to stop hating, stop now. Which is really to say that since we will die, we should die now, and act at least in part as ghosts, with their equanimity and detachment.

)

As a native Damascene, all my revelations came on the road to elsewhere. All were eclipses, all were skies falling silent.

)

The male genitals are worn externally as evolution is in the process of expelling them from the body. Another million years and they'll be stored in a drawer.

)

I can see exactly what *not* to do at the moment. No doubt through the usual process of elimination I'll arrive at my favourite strategy of total paralysis.

❧

Ego-surfing again, auto-googling, four months since I last dared: the hit-count tripled, nearly all of them name-checks by brand-new enemies, or recruits to the army of doppelgangers—champion disco-dancers, Alaskan Romanticists, men who teach juggling, fuck donkeys, or put miniature combine harvesters in bottles . . . Of whom I would have known nothing, if vanity hadn't tricked me into putting my head round this mirrored corridor of hell again. Good that at least one of our sins now carries its immediate terrestrial punishment.

❧

Everything is driven towards entropy, and yet everywhere aspires to the order still inscribed in it by our primal singularity, our cosmic egg—and falls into sphere, orbit, season and pulse. But how sad to find yourself born into a universe founded on the principle of *nostalgia*.

❧

With your back to the wall, always pay a compliment. Even your mugger or torturer is not immune to flattery, and still capable of being a little disarmed by a word of congratulation on their choice of footwear or superior technique.

❧

I wonder if anyone was ever tempted to play a trick on Helen Keller, and communicate to her that she was really dead. Then again, I once played the same trick on myself, and have done nothing but seek a minute-by-minute reassurance from everything since. So this, dear, is why I touch everyone all the time; I truly wish it *was* something as discriminating as lasciviousness. You will see me display the same overfamiliarity towards the furniture.

❧

Whale to the ocean, bird to the sky, man to his dream.

❧

No sense steps into the same word twice.

❧

The Calvinist knife-edge. Self-loathing gets me out of bed in the morning; but for years it kept me in it.

❧

After a reading in Rotterdam, a woman came up to me and complimented me on my performance. I half-heard her, and made her repeat what she had just said. 'Sorry!' I replied, 'I just wanted to hear you say it twice. . . .' My weak little joke was either lost on her, or somehow fatally misjudged; she threw up her hands in despair and stormed off. *I can now turn on a sixpence,* I thought to myself, *com-press the effect of several years of my acquaintance into a matter of* seconds . . .

❧

Poetry! What a fine thing to be working in a medium that brings out the best only in the murderous soul of the poet, and quite the very worst in everyone else. Even a limerick will dig out the one grain of ugly ambition in the heart of a saint.

❧

An afternoon watching the Paralympics, the 100m Butterfly won by a swimmer with no arms, head-butting the end of the pool in order to finish. An astonishing performance; though to my infinite shame I found myself wishing that the human spirit would sometimes triumph just a little *less*.

❧

When I was ill, I could hear the rhythmic ictus in all conversation, as clear as a snare-drum; I was as aware of the speed of the car as if the road were an inch from my own outstretched fingertips; I saw how my every human exchange took place without my conscious volition. In other words: I lost all sense of unreality.

❧

In the arts, mere reflection does for epiphany among the poor. A smash-hit piece of local theatre might consist of little more than a public recitation of their street-names and estates. They receive so little self-validation that come Friday night the mere sight of themselves seems revelatory.

❧

He spent his life paralysed by imaginary protocols.

❧

Sex is better in dreams as the prick has an eye.

❧

It is not the sophistication but the poverty of a people that is revealed by the local flourishes of their speech. The infinite Sami terms for snow (Eskimos, contrary to popular myth, have need of just two), the eighty shades of green a Nepali can summon by name, are really just the songs of thin economies, which *always* demand this kind of local hyponymic explosion—and are beautiful only to the alien eavesdropper. Scots, for example, has sixty-three words for different kinds of expectoration, being simply our traditional impediment to work. *Kechle, kisty-whistle* and *black hoast* may even sound charming to you; to me they do little more than explain the absence of our erotic literature.

❧

Please don't be misled by the apparent self-certainty of these utterances. Be assured that after each one I nervously delete the words *but that's probably just me, right* . . .

❧

As his insults were no different from those I hurl at the mirror every morning, at least my enemy did not have the advantage of surprise. But then I understood: as is so often the case with such unguarded hysterias, he had merely provided a negative litany of his own long-unacknowledged virtues. Among these, it seems we were now required to account his beauty, his originality, his grace, even his fine head of hair. And at the thought of that aging popinjay gurning before *his* mirror each morning . . . I was suddenly mortified with pity.

❧

It would be a great help to me personally if they would paint all the planes that are going to crash at some point in their service with a large black stripe. I *abhor* the way I am continually prodded into uninformed decisions.

❧

I sometimes wonder if my meditations have won me anything more than *estrangement*, the right to wake up every morning as a bald white monkey with gravity issues.

❧

No one has ever adequately explained to me the self-evident merit in sensitivity. I spent my first seventeen years feeling everything, and the only place it got me was the mental ward. There is also something base about art which provokes us merely to *suffer* more than we need to, and in doing so blunting our more sophisticated responses.

❧

That night we saw through him, all of us, and he knew it. O it was a terrible thing to then watch a man try to *substantialize* himself.

❧

What kills the writer, in the end, is the absence of a direct causal relationship between effort and reward. Thus it is rarely true *work*, in any way our bodies can understand. A free day, all the kids off to their grandmother's, the house deathly quiet; half an hour's meditation; a cafetière of Costa Rica in the study; no sound but the rain dripping from the trees in the back garden through the open window. . . . And I cannot introduce two words to one another without them falling out immediately. Today, feeling exhausted, ill, overweight, the house full of yelling, my mind a roiling broth of fear and resentment and professional jealousy—a dozen problems I have pored over for weeks have been solved in twenty minutes flat. I end the day feeling worse than ever, as if I had accomplished nothing at all.

᪑

They awoke in a dark and windowless room, and all had forgotten how long they had slept. After a month of blindness they found a torch, which some declared an abomination, and retreated to the shadows forever. Then those with a torch found a watch, which read twelve; and some decided it was midnight, and some noon, and thereafter both parties developed their separate cultures.

᪑

Remove the error of self, and being here once is the identically equivalent miracle (if you can now conscionably use such a word) to being here again. The life now is already life after death, as remarkably so as any you might live in the future. Nothing will constitute the new you except the organism whose evolution has demanded, just as yours does now, the construction of another phantom centre. The next thing 'we' will indisputably know is another reawakening, the clever self-creation of the brief soul of something or other; though we might as well face up to the fact that—our infinite vegetable slumberings notwithstanding—we'll do well to make a rat or jellyfish; more likely some bizarre phenotype a few million light-years distant. The best we can pray for is that there is a secret economy at work, whereby a presently inscrutable, quantum-tunnelled aspect of our human schooling is converted to some universal currency and smuggled over. If I'm brutally honest, though, I can assemble little evidence to offer myself that I 'got lucky' this time round, and that the experience is worth repeating. What I think of as a fondness for being human is really just an attachment to being me, that is—to nothing at all.

❧

No, I'm not obsessed with myself, just *the* self; I could be just as easily mesmerised by yours, if it were as readily available for study.

❧

Email allows me to indulge my new meditative technique: annihilation via impersonation. I answer each letter in my interlocutor's voice, and forty responses later I am no one.

❧

The truer we sing, the more we violate our own boundaries, and the more our bodies protest; those who sing truest are all suicides.

❧

My deeper ignorances I intend to cure by reincarnation. Not without its own inconveniences, to be sure, but fewer than the prospect of actual *study*.

❧

I wake up crapulous and half-suicidal in a hotel room at 6 a.m., exhausted by my sweats and nightmares. I grope for the remote, and the breakfast show. A radiant woman is being interviewed, and the caption below her simply reads *Former Sufferer* . . .

⟨

Only the best poets can risk simplicity. The rest of us are merely exposed by it. Only those same poets can risk complexity too: the rest invariably fail to realise the greatly increased responsibility towards *clarity* that it demands. Nonetheless so many rush towards it, knowing their faults are here best concealed.

⟨

The Greeks right again. The light indeed pours from our eyes—its little, dim, narrow human light: we stand before the world like a projectionist behind his dusty cone of shadows, illuminating only what we already know.

⟨

Certain events, if repeated often enough, allow their internal eidolon to be conjured at will. The fingertips on the fretboard, the slalom of the tongue on her thigh, the weight of the book, the screw on the south-westernmost quadrant of the cue-ball. . . . All these things access my realm of waking dream.

ʔ

We were strolling along the street, and passed a couple of sleepy undergraduates. Suddenly my companion interjected—*so then I shot him in the face—terrible fucking mess, brains all up the walls* . . . for no reason other than to bring a little colour into the lives of his eavesdroppers. He then resumed our conversation on Sondheim.

ʔ

In this life, only *older* holds out the genuine possibility of our not being us.

ʔ

When you respond by acting just as they do, low men immediately impute to you their own motives, and are torn between fear and camaraderie.

❢

Lessons instantly learned, and I pass this on to you urgently: better to forget a woman's birthday altogether than to guess it six months out.

❢

The laws of this particular universe favour creatures of a certain size, on planets of a certain gravity, orbiting stars of a certain optimum mass.... And so on, for twenty other non-negotiable conditions. From which we can quickly extrapolate that the bicycle and the piano are almost certainly *universal solutions.* Nothing makes me more happy or more sad than the thought of my brother or sister sitting, right now, in a room so far distant not even light can pass between us, their rooms furnished with near-identical stuff.... And dreaming, perhaps, the same cosmic solidarity—that dream, that thought, being the only thing we will ever exchange.

❢

The reason for the pillow is that it eliminates the face.

⟅

L. rather stagily 'insults my integrity', and expects me to be left reeling. I barely understood the offence. He was pulling a face at a blind man.

⟅

If I existed before this life and yet can recall nothing of it, then there is no 'I' that can be sensibly discussed beyond its present manifestation. Yet I have no doubt that I *have* existed before, simply because to say otherwise is to commit the Ptolemaic error of declaring one's present situation unique and miraculous. In this life my true family is a set with only one member; the minds of the others can be read but never penetrated. Nor can any fraternity be extended to the chain of my previous 'I's: all the links are uncoupled, and there is no lineage to pursue. Therefore my lives prior to this incarnation must encompass all the things that have ever been. Having no allegiance to any single mind, I discover myself nowhere and everywhere. My mind was there dispersed, and for fourteen billion years I partook of *all* lives, as the as-yet-uncondensed minds beyond my death

now partake of my own. This leaves my present mind as a
mere designated point, an inspissation of a universal mind
that has condensed in me for *no reason* but the one it now
chooses for itself: to uncover its own nature. I thought this
a romantic fallacy, right up to the sudden and horrified
registration of its demonstrable truth: we are matter;
thinking is what we do here; therefore we are not the slaves
but the primary agents of that universal mind. I have *sole
responsibility.*

❧

You've made a *blog.* . . . Clever boy! Next: flushing.

❧

Naturally, he had not once contemplated the possibility
that the subject of his life's study might have been an idiot.
His meticulous exegeses of the poems of X were about as
edifying as the spectacle of a great scientist performing the
microscopic dissection of a hamburger.

❧

She insisted on absolute honesty, so I told her everything. I never saw her again, but at least I had spared the next guy the same ordeal.

❧

Unthinkable that I would ever put my own happiness— whatever the fuck *that* is—before anyone else's. Alas when all the people whose happiness I had put first realised the extent of their company, they seemed considerably less touched by my selflessness.

❧

A beautiful man or woman I do not know steps with me into an empty lift, still ripe with the bad fart of the previous occupant—and I experience an immediate, specific, visceral revulsion towards *them.* The immaculate are tainted waiting to happen.

❧

He could contrive, he knew, even an inauthentic suicide; his merely staying alive was his one concession to good taste.

❧

I had never had such a thing before: a *declared* enemy. But I'd be lost without him now. It's a feeling so close to love. I *made* him, as one makes a poem or a child, by accident *and* design.

❧

If we look hard enough, we can always find both insight and beauty in meaningless verse; though we are paying no compliment whatsoever to the *poem,* but only to our own intelligence, in whose company we have merely spent a little uninterrupted time.

❧

What I find most offensive is the world's presumption that it has *rescued* me from non-existence, its . . . pleased expression.

❧

I was always pretty good at low-grade luck, those sad little two-cherry windfalls, and could always whistle up the yellow roof-light of the empty cab at three in the morning, the half-wish of the faint meteor, that wee treasurable frisson of the envelope icon on the mobile . . . But my psychic *aim* is catastrophic. There are days when I can make the phone ring at will, but it's always the last person I want to hear from. If you want some roses delivered out the blue from a secret admirer, I can probably arrange it for you, if you don't mind them being from your psychopathic driving instructor.

❧

Nightmare: that consciousness might never take another form but this phantom centre, whose presence in others we can only confirm by indirect means. I have felt myself on the verge of tearing lovers limb from limb, to find that heart I had dreamt of being lost within. . . . Were it all to be *definitively* proven—were we to know ourselves locked into the individual soul *forever*—the whole human project would fold its hand tomorrow.

❧

Faces rarely betray the true feelings of their owners, publicly or privately—with one exception: there is a tiny leakage in all acts of departure. If you attend, with preternatural care, to her eyes in the millisecond just prior to your turning your back to leave the room . . . There you will learn the very worst of what she thinks of you.

❧

From the cloud to the zip-fastener, the silver birch to the dirty bomb, everything *arose*—and so must be considered a member of the set of natural objects.

❧

Boredom, in its uncut state, is a *force.* To know it takes a mind of unassuagable restlessness—which pays that mind no compliment, as it implies neither curiosity nor any particular capacity for insight. Nor can such a mind ever disarm its own boredom by meditating upon nothing. Instead it perfects its obsession, its meditation upon *one* thing: in this we also lose the self, but bargain away the whole world too, in exchange for a profound intimacy with the Speyside malts, postage stamps, death, the feet of women.

❧

When you first make love to the beloved, you enter a zone of unfocus as your face approaches hers . . . From which she reappears, in close-up, as a stranger. With anyone *but* the beloved, the experience is smoothly gradated; but such is the beloved's conflation with our *angel,* we know they have fallen to be with us, changed their essential nature for the sake of human love. . . . And there our gratitude is bound to be mixed. Indeed, at first sight, she can look heart-breakingly close to the ugliest thing you have ever seen.

❧

Wouldn't it be wonderful to start our children's spiritual education at the age of six with the honest opener: *Children— I'm afraid no one has the first clue why we're here.*

❧

He was no fool, and yet he had written a book by a fool. As a dramatic monologue it would have been a triumph of sustained impersonation, had we not suspected that *fool* was the beginning and end of his literary repertoire.

❧

Your manifest uncertainty is the best guarantor of the truth of your statement, not your wise voice.

❧

He liked to think of himself as a thorn in our side; but he was a much smaller man than he imagined himself, and merely a pain in the ass.

❧

Doors, those merciful *conceits,* those blind eyes of the house. . . . As if your daughter or brother or friend isn't beating off or taking a shit six feet from where you stand.

❧

A medium once told me that in my previous incarnation I had been a bluebottle who had caused an accident in a private plane, in which an evil man had been killed. As a result of that inadvertent heroism I had been karmically fast-tracked, despite the opposition of several high-ranking devas. I was immediately convinced of the truth of this story, and it continues to explain everything.

❧

The fuel-injected articulacy of everything we write in infatuation or anger. Latin for the fury, love's Anglo-Saxon tropes . . . No wonder writers wreck their lives trying to maintain these two states.

❧

I have owed a slight acquaintance, K., an email for six months. This morning I hear that he has died. My single obsequy was to cross him off my to-do list, and feel my burden lighten a little. I even caught myself wondering if there might be something in this that could be worked up into a general strategy.

❧

Of all the layers of dream that govern this life, the deepest and most catastrophic is that of our solitariness; only death cures it, and even then only by cessation, not awakening.

❧

By the age of eleven, I was finally exasperated with my parents. I knew I had been left with no alternative but to fuck *myself* up.

ϟ

'Now I'll read a *funny* poem.' *Oh,* I thought. *I'll be the judge of* that.

ϟ

'Now I'll read a long poem.' And as one heart, our hearts sunk; somewhere I heard a hundred slide trombones slump weakly. It was then I finally admitted to myself that a poetry reading was *no night out.*

ϟ

The self is a universal vanishing point.

ϟ

'When I die,' he told me, 'I want every organ in my body to be completely *fucked*.' And so it was: they found his twenty-stone carcass on the sofa, soaked in spilt beer and melted Häagen-Dazs, smiling like the Buddha, and not a cell of him worth donating. As ambitions go, by no means the worst: to have exhausted the organism, to have wasted *nothing...*

❧

I could not rouse myself from the nightmare; mercifully I was not alone in bed, and she heard my muffled cries and freed me. The dream, I told her, was simply that I had no body to wake to, and hence no way out of the dream. Yet now that I was awake, it was no better. I knew I was still dreaming bodiless, and that not even death itself could spring me from it, and that all my life had been a mere diversion from this rising panic.

❧

There *is* a universal eye, but it sees only through our own: our every blink blinds it.

❧

I asked her what she thought had given our relationship its longevity, and so initiated—I quickly realised—the first discussion of our relationship we had ever had. We were finished in a month.

❧

A day lost in failed spells, trying to conjure a ring from the phone: all those miserable countdowns to nothing, to zero, to no event.

❧

No, you confuse having entertained my idea with having merely *read* it; hence the ease of your dismissal.

❧

I was so practised in disappointment, I absorbed the blow of her leaving me almost effortlessly. Allowing yourself to be *constructed* by the lover means you have been a different man from the start; I merely left his body behind like a husk, and let him take the punch. (I watched him double up, as from above.) The loveless wraith of me was then free to wander, looking for my new instructions.

❧

My plan was to involve her in an act of such intimacy as to both repel and enslave her: I had long understood the power of our disgusted complicities. But *nothing* could enslave her, *nothing* could repel her; and in reaching my own extremes I realised the game had been hers all along, and that I had lost my mind months ago.

❧

Fate's book, but my italics.

❧

Her so suddenly quitting in the early stages of our relationship meant I was obliged to hurriedly revise my future; at least this afforded me, I decided, the bravery of a blank canvas I might not otherwise have granted myself. Unfortunately, the new ventures and career-paths I proposed—street-vendor, lunatic, rapist, drunk—seemed oddly in the grip of certain imaginative constraints.

❧

Imagining the worst is no talisman against it.

❧

He was obsessed with his fallibility, and I cared not a jot for mine. This, together with my gift for instant recantation, put me at a terrifically unfair advantage.

❧

My time here has afforded me no enlightenment, though my night-vision has improved enormously. In fact it seems to have evolved as if certain of its future indispensability.

❧

With friends and strangers I can be no one; more and more
I confine myself to their company. Then one day I enter
a room full of acquaintances, and fly into a blind panic: I
cannot remember for the life of me who these people think
I am . . .

❧

He always whispered the bad news in your left ear; always
made sure his slanders were printed verso . . . For years he
escaped our attention. We knew, vaguely, that evil accom-
panied him, but thought the two no more connected than
the tree and the wind that shook it. Then one day we realised
there was no wind: just his own black whistling.

❧

I tried for a while to keep a diary, making one entry at dawn and another on the facing page before I fell asleep. (There are no meridian diaries; anyone able-bodied and under the age of seventy who has the leisure to write one is beneath contempt.) The irreconcilability of the two personalities was so immediately apparent, I quit after a few weeks. The dumb hope of one, then the disillusion of the other—a motif repeated without interruption—depressed me beyond words. I went back to bookending the days, as the human monkey should, with caffeine and alcohol, the newspaper and lovemaking, information and oblivion.

❧

All evening, listening to his wonderful table-talk, I kept finding myself think: *Ah, but in six months you'll be dead, and I will have said that . . .*

❧

He prided himself on seeing through everyone. Then one evening, at a party, I saw how his focus always fell a little too far ahead of its object; and knew he had entered the realm of phantoms.

❧

Silence between lovers always takes a negative or positive charge, and can't be empty or emptied of meaning; though if only one party understands this rule, they are in hell.

❧

A fine recording by the seventy-year-old João Gilberto, still singing beautifully at an age when nearly every other singer has gone off. . . . But there was nothing in his voice in the first place, no vibrato, no expression, nothing that could ever ripen and rot.

❧

I enjoyed L.'s creeping senility. I could have him repeat my favourite stories as often as I wanted, sometimes several times in the space of the same afternoon. X's sudden lurch into his anecdotage, on the other hand, was a disaster: until then, his shyness had prevented our discovering what a *bore* he was.

❧

In the end, the desolate age always turns instinctively to classicism, which if nothing else legislates against certain kinds of disappointment.

⸓

Language: the category error as belief-system.

⸓

The rose's night-black is as true as her day-red.

⸓

It is possible for a woman to say, honestly, that she has thought of her lover all day long—but she will neglect to mention the twenty other things she has kept in her head at the same time. A man ignorant of this ability will be terrified by her declaration, since were it to be his—it would amount to a straightforward admission of his own derangement.

⸓

As we think of the dead, so the immortals think of us: as a fraternity of ghosts, the *ones-who-pass-through* . . .

❡

Nothing more dangerous than the saviour who mistimes his appearance.

❡

Lying still inside her, I was suddenly freed from everything, my term, my fate, like a train that had run off the rails to find itself suddenly moored in the middle of a sunlit field, or a field in darkness.

❡

The bleakest and briefest of human literatures, one I have seen men read and be straightaway moved to tears: the price-tag.

❡

When I lost my virginity, I flew my *own* sheets from the
window, I *myself* bled with relief . . .

❧

Eventually most musicians give up listening to their instrument, as I did, and hear only themselves; the real musicians
never stop.

❧

The blush: what evolutionary advantage do we gain in the
publication of our embarrassment? But then the secret shame
rarely had much effect on my future conduct.

❧

You are physically closer to an acoustic guitar than any
other instrument; its body beats and moans through your
own, yes, like a lover's. Hence its attraction for losers and
loners. The singer-songwriter, of whom Orpheus is the
prototype, has his guitar primarily for company, not ac-
companiment. As he ascended from the dark, it belatedly
dawned on Orpheus that he didn't really *need* his girlfriend.

❧

I'm always amused by those commentators who nervously
insist that the working class's constant use of the word *fuck*
is really just 'a form of punctuation'. It is, however, no more
or less than what they dread: an inexhaustible river of smelted
wrath, a Phlegethon of ancestral grievance . . .

❧

I had been scrupulous in God's abolition; and nor would
I allow the humanist error of allowing his ghost to water-
mark my thinking. But then I realised that I had the oppor-
tunity to resurrect him by simply *deciding* he existed—and,
to my disgust, that there was nothing I desired as much.
There was no sophistry in this at all; since the truth was no
longer the possession of some inscrutable third party, it
no longer existed to be determined, but unilaterally decided.
I could construct whatever damn spirit I pleased. I mention
this by way of explanation, should you one day find me
torn to pieces behind the door of my locked study.

❧

Beware the obsessive between obsessions: if her brain doesn't eat itself, it will eat yours.

❡

What have the poets lost now they no longer have their mnemonics? The respect they used to arrogate to themselves through the specific threat: *Would you like me to put something in your head that you can't get out again?*

❡

The worst thing about thinking nothing of yourself is that you assume that your behaviour has no consequence. This makes you much more dangerous than the egomaniac, who at least spends all his time calculating for his own effect.

❡

Music softens us up for everything; the take-off, the poem, the needle, the bolt.

❡

What is it in the middle distance that implies our absence of attention? Short focus signs our concentration; long, our deep or distracted thought. But the eyes of the dead all converge on a point twenty yards away, presumably Death's own range.

⸎

'Trust me, you're *anything* but irresistible—' she said, 'you're just irresist*ing*.' At this she placed her hand on my heart . . . into which it appeared to sink past the wrist. The self expunged in self-disgust is just as absent as any removed by more careful means. Folk can generally go just a little deeper with me than they can with most other people before encountering the resistance of another self. This slight fall they are wont to confuse with intimacy; it's merely the reflection I offer in lieu of a personality of my own.

⸎

My friend hated book-jackets, and ripped them all off immediately. I think he felt, somehow, that the book was still trying to sell him its contents after he had paid for them. Without its dust-cover, the book is anonymous and valueless. You remove a book-jacket just as you make a lover naked: before their complete possession, they must be removed from the *currency*.

❡

The Middle American is expert in the inflation and amplification of the first person, and *dwells* on it like no one else; as in 'I'm gonna get my fat ol' lazy ass outta here'.

❡

I would hate that my Christian friend lose his faith. The dreams of the eternal agonies of his close acquaintances were his one source of real pleasure.

❡

There are nice distinctions that will ever remain a mystery to my sex. Today I asked a friend how her affair was progressing. 'It's not an *affair*,' she protested. 'We only do it in the afternoon.'

❡

Sometimes it's hard to be a guy. We can surf easily between Chomsky's home page, Teen Anal, Theravada Buddhism, and the cheat-code for *Grand Theft Auto* with scarcely a hiccup of bad conscience; the Net has externalised (and so part-socialised and normalised) a mental routine that hitherto had kept itself hidden, as we naturally assumed such ugly, unmodulated key-changes would be read as a sign of our moral degeneracy. Only an idiot would say this is a good thing, however; society is woven together by the collective denial of our nature. The leap from savannah to settlement to city was much harder for us, as our mind- and skill-sets were far less easily transferable. Had women not adapted so perfectly in a few million years, we would have cheerfully, and properly, taken another two billion over it.

❡

Everything affirms the true faith. God's indifference is as much proof of His power as His intervention. The patent uselessness of prayer is joyfully understood as the corollary of His omnipotence—by which the believer understands His arrogation of *all* the power, their own tiny allotment included.

❧

R. enters the room in a wheelchair, barely able to form a sentence, and still the light in his eyes is undimmed. I find it hard to admire such *relentless* optimism: no doubt he would describe his glass as one-tenth full.

❧

Anthony Burgess, reviewing a new edition of the *OED*, tested it by looking up his favourite *rechercherie*. He was pleased to find one particularly unusual word—but then saw that its single citation was given by Anthony Burgess. Did that supply a proof of the book's authority? Yes, if someone else looks up the word; no, if you are Anthony Burgess. Truth can be validated right up to its own front door, but no further, just as no god can confirm his own existence.

❧

The badge of the intellectually insecure is their championing of the perfectly incomprehensible, their masterly interpretations of which can never be discredited.

❧

The speed of light is only the defining *conceit* of this place. Other universes will have fallen apart in their own fashion.

❧

I had badly miscalculated: when I kicked out God, he huffily took Satan with him, whereupon went my last excuse.

❧

You are wrong about T.'s innocence being evidence of his 'good heart'; the fact that a washing machine or a toaster has no unconscious motive doesn't make it a saint.

❧

I am sent a bundle of reviews and cuttings. I can now confirm that I have a small reputation as an intelligent and wise man; I also have another as an idiot and a fool. I have a small reputation as a man capable of courtesy and discretion; I have another as a graceless and loud-mouthed buffoon. I have a small reputation as a fine and original poet; I have another as an inept and derivative one. Accounting them all, they add up, precisely, to *nothing*.

❧

First night of the flu last night. I dreamt, for what seemed like years, that I was a stand-up comedian, condemned for-ever to a disastrous routine of failed recognition humour: ... *You know every time you count from one to ten, there's always one number over? You know when you go to the Gents, and there's always that smell of creosote in the first cubicle? You know how after you come and you're bleeding from your eyes and all these fucking* dwarves *show up?* It was no more than the amplification of my waking paranoia: that I have nothing to trade, that I am anecdotally bankrupt.

❧

I wrote a blank poem once, a poem with only a title; it was immediately denounced as passé and unoriginal. But the basilisks that guard the original poems all hiss *cliché, cliché*... And sure enough, the gesture turned out to be not nearly as common as they had supposed. Indeed, a quick glance at my royalty statement tells me that it is my most anthologized piece.

❧

Went to see our new Hollywood Passion. Some kind of cultural watershed, surely: the point at which we finally succeeded in *exaggerating* Christ's agony.

❧

The doors in the carpenter's house had been so beautifully hung they were impossible to open, having created a vacuum seal around their edges. He had to remove them all then replane their sides imperfectly, so his children could get to the bathroom again. This broke his heart. Our dreams so often exceed the world's abilities.

❧

Three days of email, it transpired, had been delayed for a whole month; and for that whole month, I had been tormented by my new talent for obscure, violent and universal offence.

❧

So many of my moral crises turned out to be not my own but someone else's that I had been enthusiastically *hosting*. These proxy torments are more exhausting than any others, since one has to construct both the guilt *and* the sin.

❧

R. was so pleased with his review of my book, and could not see why I was not just as delighted. What offended me was his assumption that we publish these things and then sit around waiting for the response of him and his kind *to see whether or not they were any good*. We send these books out *believing* they're good, and would not do so otherwise. The good review doesn't fill us with joy; it only returns us to a state of equanimity. The bad drives us to despair. Thus, at the end of it all, we can never be in credit. Publication, let us never forget, is a synonym for *exposure*, a straightforward exercise in shame.

❧

God was only invented to protect the soul; the soul is just an erroneous back-formation from the ego; the ego is just an inwardly projected, spectral self-image which has arisen from the feedback loop of our individual consciousness, and that consciousness itself, only a tool possessed by a unit mammal which found itself in need of some half-decent predictive capability. In the name of which little skill we have immortalised ourselves, projected ourselves into an eternity on which we have not the slightest foothold.

₹

My parents conceived me, the universe conceived of me.

₹

I am dismantled by a male critic, and spend the weekend playing a violent video-game in invincible-god mode, arming myself only with a dinner fork; by Monday I have absolved him, and by Tuesday he is forgotten. I am dismantled by a female critic, and become hopelessly aroused, soon wholly obsessed with this woman who has taken such a specific *interest* in me . . .

₹

Of my male friends, maybe three have survived middle age with their hearing intact, and do not think almost continually and morbidly of themselves. (Well, maybe two; one died rather than face that possibility.) Nearly all the women have become less afraid. Even the childless seem to know themselves to belong to a generative species. But every man is a dead end, and he finds it out sooner or later.

❧

Foolishly, I buy a book on the strength of its cover quotes: several reviewers call it an 'instant classic'. It may well have been.

❧

Heavens, it was a challenge, but I eventually found an insult he could not absorb. I suspect he was merely *full*.

❧

People are their own blind-spots. All well-enough known, but it should be turned more often to our own advantage. For example: resubmit the work in the name of a rough anagram of the editor, and you will invariably find their opinion of it has dramatically improved.

❧

A well-judged compliment briefly confers a cloak of invisibility on the one who pays it. While you receive one, hold on to your wallet.

❧

After my ten-minute machine-gun raga guitar solo, my father threw me, gently, out of his country-and-western band. We are frogmarched from the genres by their guardians; they know that anything beyond the smallest mutations will destroy them. Postmodernism is really just a club for the turfed-out, for all those unwelcome Lamarckians, still bewildered at our failure to praise all the *leaps* they were making . . .

❧

The former members of the working classes can never quite believe themselves to be more than the sum of their good connections; too many of them assume that namedropping is one of the social graces.

❧

Terrifying, unthinkable—to realise that this universe only ever takes its form in the mind of one individual. No wonder we had to invent an all-seeing eye; the alternative was to place a near-infinite trust in one another. Without our gods to lift this responsibility, we would never have laid one stone on top of another, for fear all was phantasm.

❧

Shocking to think that of all the million words I have typed into this machine it has not understood *one* of them. Yet I would not carelessly insult it.

❧

The bare tree is still in the wind, as we are when we shed the leaves of our selfhood. Every thought slides through us like smoke through the branches.

❧

After a wretched, overlong and convoluted guitar solo, full of badly executed quotes from Coltrane and Keith Jarrett, an older musician whispered in my ear: 'Never be afraid of what's easy on your instrument.' Indeed, what's easy is what is most characteristic; what is difficult is what is against its native grain and resonant possibility. Good general advice.

❧

Poets dream within their imaginative elsewheres. In Scotland we live with very occasional illumination, so ours is actually a rather sunlit verse; by contrast, the Spanish poet is stalked by shadow.

❧

Of the classes of metaphor, the prepositional is the most culturally insidious and hard to eradicate. There are under-interrogated consequences, for example, in thinking that we always write poems 'on' or 'about' a subject. In doing so we are often just extending our imaginative hegemony in another act of fatal misappropriation. We fall *in* love; so our lover feels entitled to assume that when our feelings undergo any complex change, we have simply fallen back out again. The Greeks thought of their future as behind them, and their past in front where they could see it; how much human misery has been caused by the dumb inversion of that wholly sensible model?

ʔ

Placing ourselves in complete chaos forces the creation of a centre. For those who have lost theirs, a good tactic of last resort.

ʔ

I suspect the real 'trick'—if indeed it is a trick—with women is: a) simply to love their company, and be unable to disguise it; and b) be confident enough either in yourself or your other arrangements *genuinely* not to care over-much whether they will sleep with you or not. Feigned indifference is hopeless, and transparent. Desperation *stinks* to most women. But your visibly *not* hanging on the outcome of the evening is often a red rag to a bull.

❧

Only the mad are safe from doubt. I am always bewildered by those who regard a revised opinion as a sign of weakness; it strikes me as a fine guarantee of the commentator's sanity.

❧

It's monstrous to think of our parents having sex, because we then have to think of them conceiving *us*. . . . Hard enough to live with the exile, without replaying the scene of the eviction.

❧

Good workmen blame their tools too; there's such a thing
as a bad tool. *Really* bad workmen utter no complaint, ask
to be paid cash, and run.

§

Never let the gesture drown the sign.

§

One of the interesting things about mid-life, he told me,
is that there is a very short period where your sexual partners might be drawn from a thirty-year age range. Then one
night, purely aesthetic considerations do for one end, and
justified self-consciousness the other—the light stays off,
or the undershirt stays on—and the bandwidth shrinks by
twenty years again.

§

Our 'wonderful variety of regional accents' has been achieved by ensuring that half the population can't afford to travel more than ten miles from their birthplace. Nothing guarantees cultural diversity like geographic isolation. (The St. Kildans developed an incomprehensible form of Gaelic consisting mostly of speech impediments. Should we *rejoice* in this fact?) For the most part, this diversity can only be enjoyed by those moneyed travelers who can register the differences, which almost defines them as a class of cultural abstainer. As a *cause*, then, diversity can only be championed by those who least embody it. Not that any of this is wrong; just that we should accept that most arguments to preserve it are wholly paternalistic.

❧

My fear of flying has absolutely nothing to do with a fear of death, but on the contrary one of being *alive,* in all its precarious horror.

❧

God's joke, maybe, but he should work on his timing.
I always had the feeling the Big Bang was a little precipitate.
Nothing seemed *ready*.

❧

Your sincerity is neither here nor there. Writers sweat to
write like lunatics, and painters sweat to paint like children.
(By which I mean *talentless* children.) I know men who have
spent thirty years learning how to sound like they're playing the piano with their backsides. If just one brave pair
of buttocks had taken the stand beside them. . . . As it was,
they remained perennially oblivious to the shortcut, and
thought their time well spent. I once sat through an hour
of a man demonstrating his new technique for playing the
saxophone: he sucked instead of blew. We punished him
beautifully, however. We listened to him patiently; we gave
him *every encouragement* . . .

❧

The transcendental power of the dystopia. At the worst times in my life I have always sought to create them—socially, sexually, geographically—so that I might enact an *escape,* which might then grow into a more generalized tactic.

❧

R. has taken an *age* to die. We had reckoned on a few weeks, followed by five or six months' decent grace—then the brutal reappraisal of his work we all feel long overdue. Our frustration is starting to show, though. Any more procrastination, and we'll dismantle him where he lies.

❧

Each white page, another invitation to the mark of genius! Suckered into ruining it every time.

❧

Always plant a quiet line that critics can damn you with; this proves they were always hunting for it.

❧

How often as a child I entered that infinite realm. Yet I brought back not a single word to assuage my adulthood.

❧

Sense is the carrier-wave of truth.

❧

Writers can redeem a wasted day in two minutes; alas this knowledge leads them to waste their days like no one else.

❧

I could never keep it brief enough. I always strayed the wrong side of silence.

❧

A brilliant idea at 4a.m., so fine and original I had no need to write it down. Gone forever by dawn, of course. Proof again, if I needed it, that I carry the abyss inside me.

❧

He was starting a little poetry magazine, and asked me if I had any advice for a budding editor. The only thing I could think of was *open all the mail away from your face.*

❧

Valium and Black Label; *enjoy the flight;* the declared prospect of heavy turb over Malaga, and three hours in which to anticipate it. . . . Why, then, when I so often profess nothing but contempt for this heavy existence, this rage of the flesh? Precisely that: I have fear of dying in the wrong element because it will not properly negotiate my release: *I cannot return my weight to the air.* I wish only to render to Caesar that which is Caesar's, and dread my life being derelict in its last transaction.

❧

Making a child is the opposite of killing someone. But there are still occasions when the former is the misdeed and the latter the kindness.

❧

Such little memory as we recover from early childhood is really archaeology. In those seeds and potsherds we read the charmed domesticity of the ancient dead, moving through the day in their honeyed, eternal light.

⸰

My school-friend was incredulous: I had bought my father's old guitar with money from my Saturday job. Incomprehensible to the middle classes, of course, but the poor buy and sell from their parents and children, *to seal the money in.*

⸰

What kind of life would I have led without my glamorous double, who took all my missed opportunities? A tolerable one, for a start.

⸰

I am only too quick to credit strangers with either enormous sophistication or enormous stupidity. I flip between complete deference and complete condescension, so violently that I think of myself as two different men.

⸰

Astonishing, the number of mere acquaintances who immediately presume my confidence. If only they knew how hard my *closest friends* have had to work for it.

❧

Personality is a mask we can't prise off, but no less a mask for that; only death removes it. When we feel it lift away from our suddenly weightless faces . . . we will experience our first real moment.

❧

True zealots are betrayed by their admiration for their enemies, and their hatred of those who differ from them by one degree.

❧

The poorest are denied their nostalgias by their social immobility. Their primal territories are the ones they still inhabit. Their sweetest memories are all ungeographic.

❧

His corpse was beyond such trifling repose as mere peace. He had *left time,* and I could not help but reflect on the elegance of the move. Even my slow walk from the funeral parlour to the Tube station felt like an epileptic fit.

〄

I stopped writing when my behaviour became so extreme as to cease to be representative. If no one but you can verify the accuracy of your insight—it is, technically, barren.

〄

Anything but the truth as our epitaphs. Mine would read *His happiest hours were spent programming drums into a midi sequencer. T.'s: Nowhere was he more fulfilled than in those days he spent rearranging the copies of his own books on the shelf, readying the room for the Great Visitor he knew would never arrive. L.: His only serenity was in the silence following one of his devastating insults. B.: Without dark chocolate, her life would have been infinitely the poorer.*

〄

When I move from noun to verb I disappear from the world.
To have only worked, slept, made love—and never once to
have noticed yourself, to die still *unacquainted* . . .

❦

Between the ages of seven and twelve, I did nothing but
study origami . . . and for what? Four years ago, in a Belgian
bar, I folded Adolfo Cerceda's exquisite *Peacock* from a
ten-euro bill for a beautiful girl from Kiev. I recall Robert
Harbin's marginal comment on this model in *Secrets of
Origami*—'Now wait for the oohs and aahs'—which, being
all I have ever desired from an audience, made the palms of
my hands ache when I first read it. Anyway, the girl reacted
appropriately, I guess; she widened her eyes, she made
a little O of surprise; then she flattened the note out and
bought two beers. I *still* don't get it. I can look forward to
underwhelming my grandchildren on my deathbed.

❦

Possession by demons is only an inconvenience when they
are not fully assimilated.

❦

Speed up its evolution, and it becomes clear that the eye is not a receptive aperture but an exit wound, the catastrophic projectile fire of mind into the world.

❧

All I learnt was discretion.

❧

An exhibition of Dutch art: Rubens has everything leaning this way, or that way, with all the dynamic nuance of a Walt Disney. And then Vincent, who always understood that there are always at least three different winds in the sky, and that the hellish intricacy of their interaction is the reason we cannot hope to comprehend the motives or forces driving *anything*.

❧

I realize whatever slight physical appeal I may once have possessed has long faded, but I should have put more store by it at the time: I foolishly believed I might rely on my personality a little longer.

❦

Those wholly estranged from themselves only have two real homes: the monastery or the stage.

❦

On the clapped-out, bald-tired council bus, hurtling at 70 mph in the lashing rain down the dual carriageway. All of us calm, reading, talking, absorbed, bored—but for one terrified dog, yowling and yelping as if he is being thrashed with a stick. The one animal amongst us still able to respond *proportionately,* the only one still in possession of his sanity.

❦

Most worrying was his new habit of referring to himself in the sixth person.

❦

All those chairs and bathtubs and cars and shoes which, emptied of us, are immediately returned to absurdity. How many lonely things we make for the world.

⸖

Consciousness can no more unmask its own nature than the eye can see itself. It is contractually blind.

Don Paterson was born in Dundee, Scotland, in 1963. He works as a musician and editor, and teaches at the University of Saint Andrews. He is the author of *Landing Light*, winner of the Whitbread Poetry Award and the T.S. Eliot Prize, and *The White Lie: New and Selected Poetry*. With Charles Simic, he edited the anthology *New British Poetry*. Paterson lives in Kirriemuir, Scotland.

Best Thought, Worst Thought was designed by Rachel Holscher and set Arno Pro, a typeface developed by Robert Slimbach for Adobe in 2007. Composition by BookMobile Design and Publishing Services, Minneapolis, Minnesota.